# make room for *Bliss*

365 daily inspirations

JUDY STOFFEL LOEWEN
with
KRISTIE KELLER

## dedication

*We dedicate this book to all the
people out there looking for their Bliss,
and we know they will find it.*

Publishing-Partners
Port Townsend, WA 98368
www.Publishing-Partners.com
Copyright © 2015 by Judy Stoffel Loewen & Kristie Keller

Judy Stoffel Loewen
Certified Professional Coach, InviteChange
Associate Certified Coach, International Coach Federation

Kristie Keller, Licensed Massage Practitioner

www.makeroomforbliss.com
www.facebook.com/makeroomforbliss

All rights reserved. No part of this book
may be reproduced, stored in, or introduced
into a retrieval system, or transmitted in any
form, or by any means (electronic, mechanical,
photocopying, recording, or otherwise) without
the prior written permission of the author.

10 9 8 7 6 5 4 3 2 1
Printed in the United States of America

LCCN: 2015938538
ISBN: 978-0-9910120-8-4
eISBN: 978-0-9910120-9-1

Art: Susan Straub-Martin
Editing: Margaret Hollenbach
Typography: Marsha Slomowitz
eBook: Marcia Breece

## contents

foreword vii

acknowledgments viii

introduction ix

inspirations *Bliss* 1

encouragements *Bliss* 99

affirmations *Bliss* 174

reflections *Bliss* 289

# foreword

There are a lot of ways this book may be used, and
no way is right or wrong. Use it in any way that works
for you. Here are some ways that may be used:

Read the book front-to-back, just like any other book.

Read a Bliss each day, consecutively, starting with
the first section and going through the last.

Read a Bliss each day, randomly selecting one each
day, knowing that the Universe will have you
reading what you need to read each day.

Select a section – Inspirations, Encouragements,
Affirmations, or Reflections – that you feel
drawn to, and select a Bliss from that section.

Write your own thoughts, Bliss, questions,
or whatever in the margins or the blank pages –
or don't.

There are other ways –
choose one that works for you.

Have a Blissful life!

# acknowledgments

So many people have stood by us and helped us out while we have been working on this project. We will name just a few. Know, however, that whether you are named here or not, we so appreciate all the help you have given us.

### Judy Stoffel Loewen

Kurt and Matt Loewen – I couldn't have done it without your loving support. Thank you to the women of the Writer's Therapy and Tea group – Kindra Treloar, Nancy Meadows, Susan Hawkins, Karin Quirk, and Linda Zeppa. Your help and support have been and continue to be invaluable. Russell Harvey – your coaching has kept me moving forward and reminded me again and again that I am enough! And thanks to my partner Kristie Keller – we make a great team!

### Kristie Keller

Thank you to my beloved husband and son. Your love and support mean the world to me. Thank you also to my mom, who encouraged my writing from an early age. And thanks to my partner Judy. Your vision and spirit are the driving force that has made this all possible. You are a gem, and I am grateful to you for letting me tag along on this ride.

# introduction

We believe wholeheartedly in the idea that we are all creative, capable, resourceful, and whole. We are also practical, and understand that we don't all always feel that way. We write Bliss in an ongoing effort to capture authentic moments that spur us on in life.

The human experience is a journey, the cumulative effort of living out each day. The collection of Bliss in this book is ours – our own personal writings. We embrace vulnerability and share them with you as a way to share the human experience. There are a variety of ideas and sentiments. Sometimes we even repeat an idea, because life is like that, sometimes things bear repeating.

Our hope is that you will find comfort and even challenge in these pages, that they can be a place to pull from to get you thinking, even get you moving. You need not always agree. Noticing that your own thinking is different may even leave you feeling more grounded and motivated in the way you choose to show up in your life.

We are ever thankful to be at choice in our lives, to be works in progress, and to be striving to live with intention. We wish you the best as your life journey unfolds as well!

# inspirations

# 1

There is abundance in all things – believe it! Your success in an endeavor does not make my success in that endeavor less likely. We all bring different perspectives to our work, and that is a good thing. Celebrate everyone's successes, and appreciate what you bring to the table!

# 2

Be as kind to yourself as you are to everyone else. You know what a nice person you are – kind to everyone and everything? Don't you deserve the same treatment?

## 3

Breathing is so important – to stay alive,
to clear your head, to center yourself.
Just breathe…

## 4

Sometimes seeing how far there is to go
can be overwhelming. Look backwards
once in a while, not to dwell on the past,
but to see how far you have come.

## 5

Do you live in a world of high drama?
How is that working for you? We invite
you to choose a different way – the way of
No Drama. Sometimes the drama and the
chaos swirl around you so much that it is
hard to see the way out. Find it. Let the
drama be in the story and the music;
let your life be free of drama.

## 6

Have gratitude. No matter what your circumstances or what is happening, find something for which to be grateful. We are not saying it will always be easy. We are saying that it may change your perspective on life.

## 7

When you find yourself saying, "I can't do that," add "YET" to the sentence. Just because you can't do something right now doesn't mean that you will never be able to do it. Perhaps you can't do it because you have never tried. Open up your possibilities...

## 8

Be consciously at choice. Whether you realize it or not, you are always at choice. You may not necessarily choose what happens to you, but you do always choose how you respond to what happens to you. And since it is your choice, we invite you to know that you are making a choice.

## 9

Celebrate living in the present!
Now is all we have.

## 10

Recognize the miracles.
They are already happening;
all you have to do is see them!

## 11

Tell the Universe what you want,
not what you don't want. What you put
your attention on has a frequency,
and you will draw it to you. Choose
what you think about and ask for, so that
you are getting what you really want,
not what you don't want.

## 12

Is the glass half full or half empty?
How you look at things really does make
a difference. If you are stuck, try literally
changing your perspective: sit on the floor,
stand on a chair, go to a different room –
whatever works. Seeing things differently
can make you see different things.
Change your perspective.

## 13

Be Bold! Sometimes putting yourself out there can be a scary thing. We invite you to put aside the fear, and take the leap into being bold. There are no guarantees that you won't sometimes crash and burn. However, in the long run you may find that it is worth it.

## 14

Sometimes you just need to STOP and take a moment to get back to NOW.

## 15

Be gentle with those who are vulnerable, and we are all vulnerable. When someone honors you by being vulnerable in front of you, please treat it as the gift that it is. Vulnerability is a difficult thing for most people to share. If showing vulnerability proves to be a painful experience, it may not be shared again. And when one person is brave and shows their vulnerability, others are encouraged to show theirs.

## 16

Live an authentic life. People can tell when you are living an authentic life, and it is a reminder to them that they can do the same.

# 17

Is there too much going on in your life? Are you trying to do so many things that you feel like nothing is really getting the attention it deserves? Take action and make some room in your life. Let go of things that no longer serve you. Don't be afraid to say no. Trust your inner voice – it knows. You know!

# 18

The sun that sets on you tonight is rising on someone else, and will rise for you again tomorrow. Believe…

# 19

Today, choose to be happy. Whether you can sustain it for 5 minutes, 2 hours, or the whole day, take some time to simply be happy. When something threatens to steal your happiness, decide if you will let it. Remember, practice makes us more skillful, so go ahead and BE HAPPY!

# 20

Just show up – it is important to show up in your life. If you are having a difficult time of it, show up anyway. If all you can do is show up, then that is enough for now. Maybe something will happen, maybe it won't. But nothing can happen if you are not there.

## 21

Laugh out loud! Make sure to practice it at least once a day. If you haven't laughed much lately, start out small with a smile. Then graduate to a chuckle, and the next thing you know you will be able to produce a belly laugh on demand. Get good at it – it just may change your perspective.

## 22

We can't live in the past or the future. This is it; this is what we have to work with. NOW is all we have.

## 23

Celebrate good times. If they are happening for someone else, be wholeheartedly happy for them, and appreciate that there is good happening in the world. If the good times are yours, appreciate what you have and are experiencing, and pay attention to how you can spread those good times around to others.

## 24

GO BIG! I choose to be vulnerable and go big in all that I do this year. The only thing that can hold me back is me, and I am not willing to let that happen!

## 25

Be thankful for everything. If it's what you wanted, that's great. If it's not, maybe it's what you need to get through to what you want. Or maybe it's what you need to realize that what you thought you wanted isn't really what you want at all. There is a reason for everything – and it's not always what you think. Perspective is everything, and just maybe things will become clear later. For now, try to find gratitude for some aspect of what is happening now.

## 26

Beginnings are exciting! You get to choose what you want to spend your time and energy on going forward. Every day is a new beginning; what will you choose to spend your precious attention on?

## 27

What is the best gift you can give to yourself, your loved ones, your friends, and, in fact, the entire world? It is your authentic self. No one can be YOU better than YOU can be! It can sometimes be scary to show up as your authentic self, and it can be one of the most rewarding things you can do. Choose to show up as you, and see how it feels!

## 28

Just because you choose to see the good in people and look for the bright side of a situation does not mean that you aren't realistic. You can see the bad but choose to focus on the good.

## 29

There is abundance – but you may not experience it if you put your attention on scarcity. People are good – but you may not experience that if you put your attention on people who treat you badly. You are creative, capable, resourceful, and whole – but you may feel otherwise if your attention is on what you think you can't do. Do you see a pattern here? Choose wisely where you put your attention – it does matter!

## 30

Sometimes looking at a whole project can be so overwhelming that it can seem impossible to finish, so why start. Try handling just the amount that seems do-able at the moment, and do it.

Then celebrate the fact that the next step has been taken. The way to get things done is just one step at a time.

## 31

Dare to open up. You cannot get something new if you are holding on to something old with a tight fist. Similarly, it is good to have a mind that is open to new ideas. This is not to say that everything old should be discarded, or everything new should be embraced. You can let go of old things and thoughts that no longer serve you, and welcome in new things and thoughts that may. Dare to let go of the fear of the unknown – be open to possibility.

# 32

Pay it forward. What a great concept. The person on the receiving end feels gratitude for the unexpected kindness; the person on the giving end feels gratitude for having done something to make someone else feel good. Do it today. It doesn't have to be huge (though it can be). Pay a toll for the next car; buy coffee for the next person in line; help someone with their bags; hold the door open for someone. Do it in secret or out in the open. It doesn't matter – just do it. How does it feel?

## 33

Breathe in…Breathe out…Breathe in…
feel the feelings…all of them…pain,
anger, frustration, joy, happiness…Breathe
out…let them go. Notice them, feel them,
and don't be attached to them.

## 34

What do you say to someone who is
hurting? There is no one 'right' answer –
it depends so much on the person,
your relationship, and what happened.
Letting your heart guide you is the best
thing you can do. Sometimes the best
thing is to not say anything, just be there.

## 35

Some people make a difference in this world by doing something huge, like curing a disease or discovering something. And some people make a difference in this world by smaller actions, like listening to a child or paying for a stranger's coffee. There are at least as many ways to make a difference in this world as there are people – celebrate and be grateful for all of them. And go out and make your own difference, big or small. They are all important!

## 36

Letting go is hard…do it anyway. It doesn't matter what you are trying to let go of: self-righteous anger, children, bad habits, whatever. Even when you know it's the best thing to do, you want to do it, and you know you will be better off when it is done, it is still hard. Do it anyway.

## 37

Enjoy the present – celebrate each moment. These routine days will pass so quickly. Seedlings will turn into plants, kittens into cats, puppies into dogs, cute babies into adolescents, and adolescents into young men and women. When you are in the middle of it, some days seem to last forever and the stages go on and on. However, when you are looking back on it, it has gone by so fast that it is all a blur. Cherish the NOW, while you have it.

## 38

Spontaneous Dance Party!
Have you ever stopped what you are doing, cranked up the music, and indulged in a spontaneous dance party? Do it now! Go ahead...belt out the lyrics if you like, and be sure to shake your groove thing! Now how do you feel?

## 39

There is beauty in all things...from a baby's giggle to a grandma's wrinkles; from a beautiful flower to a sea-worn pebble. See the beauty around you!

# 40

If you are feeling down about something,
try to pinpoint what it is that is making you
feel that way. Acknowledge your feelings,
and then move on. Allow yourself to feel
what you feel; just don't allow yourself to
wallow in it – at least not for very long.
Throw yourself a five-minute pity party.
And don't forget to move on.
Find something that makes you smile,
that brings joy into your life. And be
done with what is done.

# 41

Stop and be still, at least once a day.
Do it more, if you can manage it.
In our busy and hurried lives, this isn't
always an easy thing to do. And yet it
is a very important thing to do.
In the stillness you can find your
connection to the Universe, or God,
or the Cosmic Consciousness, or You,
or whatever you call that inner voice.
In the stillness you can find Peace.

# 42

Make your decisions and move on.
Remember that very few choices in
this life cannot be changed later.
You are constantly being bombarded
with new information. Don't let this
onslaught of information paralyze you.
Make your decisions today with the
best information you have today,
and tomorrow do the same.

inspirations

## 43

Go out looking for the good; it IS there.
The bad will always be with us, and is
so much easier to find sometimes.
So go identify the good and celebrate it –
the abundance, the beauty, and the
small kind acts. Rejoice in the good!

## 44

Are you having a hard time letting go
of something that happened in the past?
It doesn't matter what it is: something you
did to someone else, something someone
else did to you, a real or perceived slight.
Let it go. Inhale: forgive yourself for your
part in it and forgive anyone else for
their part in it. Exhale: release it into the
Universe. Inhale and Exhale. Repeat.

## 45

Celebrate YOU! You are a spectacular, unique individual, and you are doing a great job!

## 46

Find a way to do what you love. Do it for a living or do it as a hobby; do it full-time or part-time. Do it for a lot of money, for a little money, or for free. What you get paid for doing it does not define it or you. Doing what you love will bring you joy, and joy is good for you!

# 47

One of the most useful abilities we can cultivate is the art of disagreeing with someone without being disagreeable. There are always things that people are not going to agree on, from the mundane to the epic. It is so important to remember that everyone is entitled to their own opinion; there is rarely a 'right' answer. Stating your opinion in a manner that sounds like it is the only truth can make people unable to hear what you are actually saying. Try stating your opinion in a way that is meant to share what you think, rather than convince everyone that you are right. Learn to disagree without being disagreeable.

## 48

Sometimes we get so mired in the mundane stuff of life that we don't see the wonderful things coming our way. Look for them! It may be a butterfly crossing our path, or finding a ten-dollar bill in the pocket of something we haven't worn for a while. Or it could be running into an old friend we weren't expecting to see, or a cancellation that leaves us unexpectedly free for an hour. It could be any number of things, and if we aren't watching for the good stuff, we may miss that it happened.

Anticipate the good things coming your way, and watch for them!

## 49

Do something nice just because you can, every day. Whether it is something nice for you, or something nice for someone else, or something nice for you because it is something nice for someone else, just do it.

## 50

It is easy to compare woes. It is courageous to admit your true happiness. Dare to be different; let the struggle go.

# 51

You hear it all the time, because it is true.
Savor each and every minute with the
people you love. You don't know how long
you or they will be here. They may move
or get involved with things that don't
include you, or they may pass –
anything can happen. What is meant
to be WILL be. Don't find yourself
in the position of saying, "if only..."
If there is something that is important
to do or say, then do it or say it now.

# 52

One of the hardest things you have to do as a parent, a spouse, or a friend, is to realize that you are not here to make people's decisions for them. It can be frustrating to watch someone you love do what you consider to be "all the wrong things," or nothing at all. You may think that things are very clear, and that there is a right and a wrong way to do things. Remember that no matter how close you are to someone, and how much you love them, they still have their own path to walk. It may be very unclear to you – it may even be very unclear to them – and it is their life's work to figure it out. Live your life in the best way that you can, and let others travel their own path.

## 53

Are you reacting to what is actually happening, or to the story you are telling yourself about what is happening? Don't assume that you know what the motivation or back story of an event is; it can make things seem much worse than they are. For instance, if your partner is aloof and not speaking to you, don't assume that it is about you. Feelings of insecurity that come out at times like these are not helpful at all. Instead, why not ask? You can always try, "The story I am telling myself about this is (fill in the blank), can you please tell me if I am correct?" In the unlikely event that you are correct, then at least you know. And in the more likely scenario that you are not correct, then you also know. Don't assume; ask the question.

## 54

Be gentle with everyone you come into contact with, for you have no idea what kind of burdens they carry. And don't forget to be gentle with yourself as well. It can be easy to forget that you also carry burdens that others can't see. It is truly a wonderful thing to be there for someone else, and it is even more awesome to be there for yourself. Being harsh with yourself will eventually wear you down, leaving you with no resources. By taking care of yourself, you allow yourself to have the ability to take care of others.

## 55

Did you forget someone's name, or your best friend's birthday? Are you embarrassed because you don't know what is being talked about? Are you afraid to ask because you feel you SHOULD know?

There IS a solution to this – just ask! Swallow your pride, admit that you don't know, and ask. You may actually be doing others a big favor by letting them see that it is okay not to know something. Forget about what you SHOULD know, and ask for the information so that you DO know.

## 56

It's not always an easy thing to do, but try to assume the best intentions behind the actions of others. No matter how clumsy or misguided something appears to be, often the intentions were good.

*inspirations*

# 57

Say what you mean. Sometimes it feels like the best thing to do is say "Maybe" or "I'll think about it," when what you mean is "No." This may seem like the polite and easy way of saying no, but it leaves the door open to a possible yes. So if you really mean you want to think about it, say "I'll think about it." But if you really mean "No, because I don't have time/can't/don't want to," then politely say "No" the first time, and be done with it. It gets it off your plate, and allows the person asking to move on.

## 58

When you are feeling down and a little funky, here's a pretty sure way to get out of it. Reach out to someone. Whether it is to make a connection for yourself, so you don't feel so alone, or to help someone else out, it is a recipe for lifting yourself up.

## 59

Everyone is in my life for a reason. I may learn from them or teach them – or both. Some may please me; some may aggravate me. To each I say: I bless you and appreciate what you bring to my life.

# 60

It's not always about you, you know. It's not a bad thing to look at what you are doing or saying, and to be honest with yourself about your part in some situation, but being honest with yourself is the key. Don't beat yourself up over things that you have no control over and no responsibility for. Sometimes it's not what you said or did; it's just not about you. Don't take it personally!

# 61

What is the one thing that I say every day, no matter what has happened? When the day has been a total disaster, I say Thank You because I made it through. When the day has been full of lovely things, I say Thank You for the beauty. When I have accomplished crossing things off my list, I say Thank You for the ability to get things done. When I have no words for anything else, I say Thank You!

# 62

We hear it all the time: life is fleeting, you never know how long someone you love will be here. And it is true. Too often people leave us and we feel that they didn't know how much we love them. We think that there is always tomorrow, but sometimes there isn't a tomorrow. Let the people in your life know now, and often, how you feel about them. Say I love you to your kids who think it's corny. Say I love you to the person you don't say it to, because you know that they know. Say it to your friends. It will still be hard when someone leaves this earth. And you will know that they knew they were loved, because you told them.

## 63

Sometimes I just want to yell out, "I am dancing as fast as I can!" Life gets hectic; there is too much to do, and it often all needs to be done at once. At times like these, I need to remember to stop, inhale, exhale, and repeat. Breathing is important – remember it!

## 64

Reality is what is happening now – it is what it is. Understand that it doesn't always have to be this way, but realize that you can't change something you refuse to acknowledge. Accept reality for what it is, in order to effect change on it.

## 65

We are all doing the best we can with what we have and what we know right now. It is easy to look back and think, "I should have known and done better," but if you really had known better you probably would have done better. Don't beat yourself up over what has happened in the past. The past is done; you can't change it. What you can do is learn from it, so that next time you will know and do a little better.

## 66

Appreciate what you have, and more will appear. Good things happen!

# 67

Try something new. There is great joy in a child's face when they have mastered something new, and when they figure out they can do it, they do it over and over again. That's what I wish for everyone – that feeling of deep, abiding joy when you master something new. You don't have to be perfect at it, you just have to have done it! Go out there and try something new today, and don't worry about being perfect, just master the first step – the rest will follow!

inspirations

# 68

Sometimes we say yes to things that seem perfectly do-able, and then something changes: people you were counting on drop out, someone gets sick, life happens. Don't get overwhelmed and try to take it all on yourself – ask for help. I am sure you've heard that saying, "Don't let them see you sweat." Here's a thought – sometimes it IS okay to let them see you sweat; let them see that it isn't necessarily easy. Don't get me wrong, I am not saying you should make it look any harder than it is. Just be honest with people, and ask for the help you need.

## 69

You know that thing you've always wanted to do? You should do it! What are you waiting for? Are you afraid to try to learn something new because you might look funny, or sound bad, or do it wrong? Who cares! Learn something new just to learn it. Forget about being the best, or doing it perfectly – just believe in yourself and have fun!

## 70

The antidote to everything seems to be gratitude. When I am ornery, annoyed, disillusioned, angry, put out, or just out of sorts, remembering what I am grateful for helps to pull me out of my funk. Try it – gratitude works wonders.

# 71

There are few, if any, absolutes in life. Having a plan is so important, and it can be important to be spontaneous and move ahead without a plan. Delaying gratification can be a really good thing, and it is important to not always wait for later to enjoy things. Having your goal always in mind can be good, and it is important to savor and enjoy the journey. In short, so many things are important, except when they're not. Life is about being flexible and keeping your balance.

## 72

Be aware of what you are looking for in the world, for you are sure to find it. If you are looking for all the ways that life is unfair, you are sure to pick situations that prove this fact. If you think that everyone is judging you, and you're looking for examples of it, you are sure to find them, whether they are real or imagined. When you look for the bad in people, you will see the bad in people. We are not suggesting that you ignore these things and pretend they don't exist. Be realistic and realize that the world is less than ideal. Then be sure to look for the good, because there is a lot of good that will remain hidden if you don't watch for it.

# 73

Yesterday I knew I was enough; today, not so much. Life is like that; your confidence comes and goes, things you were sure of yesterday don't seem so sure today. This is how life progresses, so know that it is normal, and there is nothing wrong with you. It is that age-old dance we all do – two steps forward and one step back. And the net result is forward movement, so embrace the dance and enjoy the journey.

# 74

Is it time to just let go? If you are having a hard time doing this, try asking yourself this question, and then answer it as honestly as you can: What am I getting out of this struggle? Perhaps when you find the answer to that question, you will be able to let go of the struggle.

## 75

Be fully present now. Are you stressing so much about what has to get done that you aren't enjoying the moment that is happening right now? Are you worrying so much about the future that you don't even see the present? Are you spending your time fretting about the past, second-guessing what you did or didn't do? One of the antidotes of stress, worry, and regret is to live in the moment. Be fully present to and appreciate what is happening right now. What needs to get done will get done, and what has already been done or not done can't be changed. Start spending your time in the present moment.

make room for bliss

## 76

Breathe, just breathe. Exhale all the doubts, confusion, guilt, and bad feelings; inhale light, love, compassion, energy, and abundance. No matter what happens, just keep breathing!

## 77

The best gift you can give to anyone is yourself: your time, your presence, your listening ears. Put down your cell phone, forget about what hasn't gotten done yet, and just be with the person you are with.

inspirations

## 78

We are all doing the best we can with the circumstances we are presented with. How about if we all just cut each other a little slack?

## 79

Smile at someone. Tell someone you love them. Tell a stranger they're doing a great job. Ask someone how they are, and really listen to the answer. Pat a co-worker on the back. Let someone know they make a difference. Tell people you appreciate them. It doesn't take a lot to make someone's day.

# 80

Look for the good, and you will find the good. Expect the unexpected, and it becomes the expected. You will manifest what you put your attention on. Be careful where you put your attention.

# 81

Do you know the best way to keep your big project moving along? It doesn't matter what it is – just take it one step at a time. It really is the only way to do anything. It is how you take a huge journey, it is how you get any project done – one step at a time. And if you have a setback, that's okay; just figure out where you are, and take that next step.

*inspirations*

## 82

I stop the negative self-talk that keeps me from doing things that I want to do. I am not talking about that inner voice that comes from my heart and guides me through life, but rather the chatter in my head that says I am not good enough, strong enough, smart enough, or anything else enough to do something. I recognize it for what it is, move through my fear, and follow through with my intentions.

## 83

Nobody owns the truth. What is true for one person is not necessarily true for another. And it is important to remember that if someone believes something different than you do, that does not make them wrong and you right, or vice versa. It is important to share ideas and speak your truth. Just remember that your truth is just that – YOUR truth.

## 84

Assume the best in people. You may be occasionally disappointed, but not always. People tend to live up to your expectations, so expect the best and appreciate the many times people come through for you. And when they don't, remember that none of us is perfect, and that we are doing the best we can at this point in our journey.

# 85

Celebrate the small things: a good cup of coffee, finding a parking place, ten minutes all to yourself. Things don't have to be large to be celebrated!

# 86

If you are agonizing over a decision, you may want to stop and ask yourself, "Will it matter in 5 years?" If the answer is no, then maybe you can make that decision and move on, knowing that this one isn't a game changer and really doesn't require more energy.

## 87

Sometimes it is enough to just be there for someone. You don't have to have the answers. Sometimes they won't even know what the questions are. Just be there, and let them know that you care.

## 88

Making a change can seem like a huge undertaking. Remember that you don't necessarily have to make that change all at once. Instead, choose one small thing to change, and then another, and then another. Eventually you will see that a lot of small changes turn into a big change.

How do you eat an elephant?

One bite at a time.

## 89

Relax. Things will be what they will be,
regardless of how much you worry about
them. Do what you can do, and then
know that worrying will not affect
the outcome, so don't!

## 90

Trying to be authentic in this crazy world
is not always easy. Pat yourself on the back
for trying, even if you fall short sometimes.

## 91

Know when it is time to stop your
brain and listen to your heart.

## 92

If you want people to really hear what you say, then you have to really say what you mean. Be direct. Don't beat around the bush, don't be passive aggressive, and don't assume anything. You will be doing yourself, as well as them, a favor.

## 93

There are always people out there who will want you to change your mind. Do your due diligence, make up your mind, and move on. The decisions in your life are yours to make. If you listen to your inner voice, you will make the best decision you can make at the time, with the information you have. You really can't ask any more of yourself than that.

## 94

I don't know if there really is a secret to a successful life, but if there is, maybe it is this: Stop looking for the secret to life, and start living your life in the best way that you can, every minute of every day. And when you fall short of your own expectations, then pick yourself up and start over again, living your life in the best way that you can, in that moment.

## 95

Do something totally unexpected to surprise someone today. It doesn't have to be a big deal – an unexpected text or phone call could totally make someone's day. Just let someone know that you are thinking about them, and bring a smile to their face.

# 96

What do you do when you find out that someone you are getting to know has beliefs or values that oppose your own?

Do you stay as neutral as possible and become curious to learn more about their point of view? It's an interesting practice. Suspending judgment is really an effort to keep an open mind. An open mind allows us the opportunity to be life-long learners. It is not necessary to shift your own beliefs or values to learn more about someone else's. In fact, you may walk away feeling a deeper connection to your own. Then again, you may have learned something new that you integrate into your own life.

## 97

You are constantly making choices
whether you are aware of it or not.
Sometimes you make a choice simply
by not making a different choice.
You will live with the consequences
of your choices, whether you made
them consciously or not. Be aware
of the choices you are making.

## 98

Life is not just about the destination.
Enjoy the journey!

# My own Bliss

make room for bliss

inspirations

encouragements

## 99

BE Authentic! Just in case you haven't heard it in a while, you matter a whole lot! Do what you can, when you can, to be all of who you are. Bring it!

## 100

I remember when 'what' I wanted to be when I grew up seemed like the most important question. Then I realized that 'who' I wanted to be was so much more significant. What we do is something to consider, but who we are being while we're doing it is the stuff of character. Dance to your own drum!

# 101

Does a decision ever seem so tough that you get almost paralyzed trying to make it? Do you feel like there is so much to consider and so much to know before you make it? At times like these, consult the experts, read the literature, and do everything you can to be sure you know as much as you can. And then remember a couple things: no one knows it all; and the experts may be the experts, but in the end, it is your life and your responsibility. You make the best decision with the information you have, and you move on. You cannot beat yourself up over information that wasn't available to you at the time the decision had to be made.

# 102

I have decided that the 'right' time is now.
Now is the 'right' time to wear my bathing
suit, use the good china, have people over,
appreciate what I have and who I am, and
love me. I am no longer going to wait for
the 'right' conditions before I do things.
You know – until I lose some weight, there
is a really special occasion, the house is
cleaner, and I am a better person.
If I wait for all my conditions to be met,
I could very well be waiting forever!
Now is all we have, and I am going to
start using it, well...now!

# 103

BE Audacious! Being bold can be fun! It is a reflection of our beliefs and our humility when we choose to act confidently.
So stand tall and make your move.

# 104

Namaste – The Light that is within me recognizes the Light that is within you.

# 105

You are exactly where you are supposed to be, and you are supposed to be exactly where you are. If you feel like you are still searching for your path, consider that 'searching' may BE your path right now.

## 106

Patience: this is one of the hardest things I have ever attempted to master, and I am not there yet. We would all be wise to develop this, as there are few situations in life where it is not needed, and it makes the wait so much easier.

## 107

Pay attention to your inner voice. You DO know; it's time to realize your truth.

# 108

**YOU ARE TRULY AMAZING!**

The Universe is not waiting to appreciate you until you become something 'more' or 'different.' The Universe appreciates you right here and right now for what you currently are. Take a tip from the Universe and celebrate YOU, because YOU are truly amazing!

# 109

I wish you peace in your soul.

## 110

BE Vulnerable! Being open to experiencing life in its entirety is not an invitation to get stuck in either joy or pain. Instead it is about movement and growth. Work with your feelings; they are yours and they are important. Roll with it!

## 111

Today is a new day; you get to choose who and how you will be in this new day. If you weren't quite who you wanted to be yesterday, go ahead – choose to be someone totally different. Or be exactly the same, or anything in between. It is your choice to make, and only you can make it.

# 112

Trust your heart. You are going to come across situations where you don't know what to say – where words just totally fail you. Don't shy away from those situations; they may be the times when you are needed the most. Your presence and compassion may be the most appreciated gifts. Just being there can help to ease the way. Trust your heart.

# 113

You are AWESOME.

## 114

When everything seems to be falling apart, when nothing is going the way you want it to, remember that the only constant in this world is change. If you don't like how things are going, wait a bit…they will change. And also remember not to get too comfortable with things if they are going as you want them to…they also may change. So do the only thing you can, whether things are going your way or not – keep on keeping on.

## 115

Be comfortable with yourself.
Do the things that you know are right
for you, and that bring you peace.

# 116

Find the joy in your day. It is just as likely to be in something small as something big. It may be right out there in front of you, or you may have to search for it a little. Go ahead – take a look. It will be worth it.

# 117

Sometimes we all get stuck in that "2 steps forward – 3 steps back" dance that makes us feel like we are going nowhere fast. It can be discouraging to feel like any forward momentum we have is canceled out by the subsequent backsliding. I don't know that there is anyone who is immune to it; it happens to everyone at some point. And it will eventually stop; a time will come when it is "3 steps forward – 2 steps back" and then "lots of steps forward and only an occasional step back." It may help to remember that it is, after all, just a temporary interlude in which we get to practice our dance steps.

## 118

Make a habit of looking for the miracles in your life. You may be surprised at how many you find when you start looking for and expecting them.

# 119

Be gentle with yourself. Unwanted things come to all of us at some point or another. Try not to let it define you – you are not what happens to you. If you need time away from other people, take it. If you need to talk about it, find someone you trust and do it. If you want suggestions, say so. If you don't want suggestions, also say so. And also be gentle with those around you, because they will want to help and may not know how.

# 120

Do what makes your heart sing!

# 121

When you dig real deep looking for what is holding you back, very often what you finally find is fear. Naming that fear and figuring out where it came from can go a long way toward helping you let go of that fear. And sometimes you find that the fear is a remnant of when you were a child, and it was trying to keep you safe. Embrace the fear, thank it for trying to keep you safe, let it know that you are now grown up and can handle things, and send it out to play.

# 122

You're not playing big if you are not all in, and you are not all in if you are not willing to be vulnerable. It's scary, and it is not fun to get hurt. Yet, if you are not willing to be open enough to get hurt, you will not be open enough to receive your biggest and best blessings. You are resilient – be brave – PLAY BIG!

# 123

Good things are coming! Sometimes I can feel it in my bones; sometimes I just have to rely on faith and believe. I don't know when, and I don't know how, but I do know.

## 124

Sometimes it's important to be the catalyst. You can hope and pray things are going to change, you can wish with all your might, but sometimes the power behind the change is in you. Do something to move toward the change you desire. Be strong, do what you do in love and with the best of intentions, and be that catalyst.

## 125

In times when you are feeling a little unsure on this journey through life, remember this: the Universe believes in you, and I believe in you. Now BELIEVE IN YOURSELF! You can do it!

# 126

Listen with your heart. When you ask someone how they are and they say "fine" or "okay," listen closely to see if there is something behind that. Sometimes people say "fine" and they mean fine. Sometimes people say "fine" and they mean "if only I had someone to talk to." But do ask; don't assume. Maybe you are that person they can talk to, and maybe you aren't. Listen with your heart and you may hear the difference.

# 127

You are incredible!
Have an amazing day!

## 128

Walk your own path. Don't let someone else choose your path for you. Even wandering around looking for your path is part of being on your path. Others may think they know exactly what you should be doing, but it is your life to live the best way that you can. Choose your own way. And if you get down the road and want to change directions, then choose again.

## 129

With every breath you take and every good thought you think and every kind word you speak, joy is spread.

# 130

The Universe rejoiced the day you were born, and we all live in appreciation and gratitude every day you are here!

# 131

Choices are hard. And sometimes, when we feel paralyzed by our choices, we just opt to not make a choice. But here's the thing: refusing to make a choice is actually making a choice by default. It is better to consciously make a choice – good, bad, or indifferent – than to let a choice make itself.

## 132

Stop beating yourself up over what you're
not doing, and start looking at what you
are doing. Are your intentions good?
Are you following your heart? It is enough.
You are enough.

## 133

I always rally for myself and the
energy to celebrate each day!

## 134

Be the YOU that you want to be someday,
NOW!

## 135

You can do it! Circumstances are the external environment. Who you are comes from within. Set your intentions on feeling like you've arrived (whatever that means for you), and see what happens.

## 136

You are a beautiful soul; don't let anyone tell you any differently!

## 137

It's a great day to become acutely aware of your blessings. Make a list, but be sure to have a lot of paper!

## 138

On days when the only action you can take is to put one foot in front of the other, remember that it is enough.

## 139

When you are in a state of overload and overwhelm, stop and take a minute to remember to live your life. Life is not something that you look forward to getting to someday. It is what is happening right now – in front of your eyes. So yes, as cliché as it sounds, stop and smell the roses. Tell the people you love that you love them. Take care of yourself. Work toward the life that you want, and live the life that you have now!

## 140

You are absolutely stunning when you are being true to yourself! Carry on.

## 141

Don't wait. The world needs you now – not when you are thinner, better, less busy, more capable, or anything else. Accept and embrace who and what you are right now, jump in with both feet, and be here for the world!

## 142

Forgiveness is important, and the first person in need of forgiveness is you. Forgive yourself for all missteps, slip-ups, moments of nastiness, less-than-ideal actions, and falls-from-grace, actual or perceived. Then forgive anyone else in your life who needs it. We are all doing the best we can with the knowledge we have at the time. Remember, forgiveness is something we do for ourselves that allows us to let go of the past and continue to live in the present.

## 143

Gratitude is the attitude to have. Every morning I wake up and rejoice in the many, many blessings that I have. Every night I go to bed and count and appreciate the many, many things that I am thankful for. Starting and ending the day with gratitude makes for a great day, no matter what happens!

# 144

You being you is what the world needs, just like it needs me being me. We are not the same, and we were not meant to be. We look different and act different. We may believe the same things, or some of the same things, or none of the same things. It doesn't matter. What matters is that we respect each other and remain true to ourselves. Don't try to be me, or anyone else. And I won't try to be you. We will each be authentically who we are.

make room for bliss

# 145

Go ahead – make a mistake! Making a mistake is not the worst thing that could happen. Doing nothing because you are afraid to make a mistake is a tragedy. Living your life in fear is a tragedy. You can recover from a mistake; you might be able to turn that mistake into something great. You can even laugh at your mistakes. Living in fear of making a mistake could result in you doing nothing, and then not only you, but the world, will never know what might have been. Go ahead – don't be afraid to make a mistake!

encouragements

## 146

It doesn't take much to be ridiculously happy: a good night's sleep, getting your garbage to the curb in time for pickup, finding the perfect color of paint for your room. Of course, be happy when the big things happen in your life. But don't wait for the big things; celebrate and rejoice in the numerous small miracles that happen every day.

## 147

Believe! Believe in people; believe in God; believe in fate; believe that everything will turn out okay; believe that you are where you are supposed to be; believe in the Universe; believe in good music; believe in the premise that people are good at heart; believe that you know; believe in miracles; believe in abundance; believe in beauty; believe in gratitude; believe in laughter; believe in yourself. Just believe!

## 148

Reach out for help. Yes, you are strong and can handle a lot, but that doesn't mean that you wouldn't benefit from a kind word or touch, or by telling your story to someone who will really hear what you are saying. You don't have to do everything by yourself.

# 149

Expect the miracles! Did you ever consider that the reason you don't see the miracles may be that you don't look for the miracles? Miracles are happening all the time; they may be large or small, but they're there. Try this out for a month: expect the miracles, and look for them. And if you decide to keep a notebook, you may want to make it a large one!

# 150

Things are getting busier; it seems that there is so much to do and so little time. Don't forget to schedule 'you' time into your days! Take some time every day to recharge your own battery. With so much to do, it may seem unlikely that you will find the time, but remember, like a battery, if you don't get recharged, you will no longer have any energy to do everything that you want to do. It is important; YOU are important!

## 151

BE Powerful! It IS possible to move through the world embracing your talents while being humble. We are often told that we can't be both confident and humble. Those are called limiting beliefs; your inner fire can override them. Onward and upward, my friend!

# 152

You are entitled to your feelings; your feelings are your feelings. Whether or not you act on those feelings is your choice. Remember that there are consequences to actions, some of which you may like and some of which you may not like. Acting on your feelings does not give you a free pass to hurt others. You are entitled to your feelings, but you are not necessarily entitled to act on them.

## 153

Be empowered by the ability to choose. The level of satisfaction you feel from your life is yours alone. Having others make choices for you so that you don't have to deal with your feelings does not change the way you are going to feel when things play out. Own it, decide for yourself, and grow as a result of it. Be someone who can look into the mirror, deep into your own eyes, and know that you are capable.

## 154

Celebrate the uniqueness of you! You are one of a kind, and the Universe needs you to be the best YOU you can be! Nobody else can be YOU, so step up!

## 155

Sometimes the hardest thing to do is to believe in yourself. Believe that you do know the best thing for you to do. Listen to the experts and then trust in yourself. The experts are the experts in their fields, and YOU are the expert in your life!

## 156

BE Forgiving! We all fall short of our best selves at some points in our lives. Be forgiving of others' shortcomings, and especially be forgiving of your own.

## 157

Choose what you want, then set out to get it. The Universe will put things in your path that will get you to where you want to be, and YOU have to choose them. It is not enough to wish for what you want; you must also act on the opportunities presented to you. You are not meant to be a passive player in your life.
**GO GET 'EM TIGER!**

## 158

You are spectacular, just the way you are. There is no one who is more you than YOU! Allow the space for others to be themselves, and make sure to allow the space for you to be YOU as well.

# 159

What if the obstacles were really life-force builders? Power up!

# 160

Enjoy Nature! The wind whispers, birds sing. Things are sprouting and beams of sunlight break through the clouds – little kisses of warmth on my forehead. Enjoy some time outside today. Even a few minutes to listen and feel what Mother Nature has to offer can do wonders for the soul.

# 161

Go ahead. Do what you need to do.
You've got this!

# 162

Life is a series of choices. Trust yourself to make a choice, commit to it, and move on. Sometimes you are going to like the result, sometimes you aren't. Most of the time you can decide to choose differently in the future. Just remember that the choice is yours to make, and not making a choice is actually letting someone else choose for you.

# 163

You may not realize it, but you are in the perfect place at the perfect time. You know that person you just smiled at? That may be the smile that makes them realize life is not as bad as it seems to be right now. And that person for whom you just held open the door? You just gave that person hope that there are, indeed, some people in this world who are paying attention and willing to help out a stranger. Sometimes it is the little kindnesses that make life bearable for people. You were the one who was there, and you were the one who made a difference.

## 164

BE Kickass! Sometimes it is important to get out there and be seen and heard. Sometimes it is important to let people know you are there and paying attention. When it is appropriate, don't be afraid to get out there and kick a little ___!

## 165

It is okay to not be blissful every minute of every day. Sometimes it is hard to find the good going on in your life, and to be grateful for that good. Try to remember that there is good – there is always good – and don't beat yourself up if you have a hard time finding it. We are all entitled to a down day! Just keep looking, eventually you will see the good!

*encouragements*

# 166

I remain open to the possibilities and realize that I will be okay. Okay may not look like what I thought it would, and that is also okay. My plans may have to change a bit, and that is not necessarily a bad thing. I will be okay!

# 167

When you are headed into those dark and fearful moments, which we all face, think of the things that you are doing to help make things better. By being proactive you can and do have an effect on your situation – you are not helpless. Remembering that you are not helpless can help take the edge off the fear.

## 168

Don't forget to give yourself credit for what you are doing. It can be as simple as putting one foot in front of the other and moving forward (which may not always feel so simple), or something that seems more daunting. Whatever you are doing, you deserve credit for it.

## 169

Sometimes the journey includes stopping to put your feet up, and resting for a spell.

# 170

It is time to go out there and be the totally awesome you that you are. By being your authentic self, you become a shining light for the world to see, and an example of the fact that we all can and should be our own authentic selves. Go ahead – jump in there and be yourself. You won't be the first, as there are some brave souls out there leading the way. You will, however, be adding to the increasing number of souls who are realizing that being anything but your authentic self is just no longer a tolerable way to live.

# 171

This year remember to look for the good – in your friends, in your family, in humanity, in your situation. There is good out there, and you will see it if you look for it. If you do not look for the good, you will be bombarded by the bad. Bad news sells, and is easy to find. And for every bad thing that makes the news, there are many good things that never will, because it is easier to sell the bad. So start looking for the good – you may be amazed at how much you find!

# 172

If you know a change is in order, make it.
There are a multitude of paths to get from
here to there, and the path you choose
may not be the same as anyone else's.
Your life does not have to make sense
to anyone else but you!

# 173

You CAN do it! Yes it is hard, and yes
it is scary. And you have the power,
the perspicacity, and the perseverance
to do what you need to do.
YOU CAN DO IT!

My own *Bliss*

make room for bliss

encouragements

# affirmations

## 174

I am grateful for what I have
and for who I am.

## 175

I do what I can to show those
around me that they are significant!

## 176

As the sunlight kisses my cheek,
I remember that this human experience –
all of it – is precious.

## 177

I am…imperfect, and that's okay.

## 178

I embrace all of my feelings. I do not
need to keep my game face on all of
the time and act as if everything is always
fine, nor do I need to create drama.
I allow myself to be sentimental,
to feel deeply, and to deal.

## 179

I breathe. I inhale calm, and exhale chaos.
I inhale knowing, and exhale doubt.
I inhale courage, and exhale fear.

## 180

I am alive from my head to my toes,
thankful for this new day, and ready
to meet all it brings!

## 181

If you are feeling inadequate and not up to par, we invite you to stop comparing yourself to others and remember this mantra: I am enough, right here and right now. I do the best that I can, right here and right now. I appreciate who I am and how far I have come. I AM ENOUGH!

## 182

I believe in miracles.

## 183

I am a spiritual being enjoying this physical experience.

## 184

Today I will do one thing better than I did yesterday. I will take one more step toward something that I want. I will not say "I can't," but will instead say "I don't know how yet." I will not look too far into the future trying to guess how long I can do something. One day at a time is my new mantra. I can do anything for a day. And that day is today.

## 185

Life is good. I appreciate
the simple things.

# 186

I am good enough. Yes, there is definitely some perfectionism in me. I want to do everything perfectly – the best, in fact. I can get so wrapped up in trying to be brilliant that I become paralyzed. I sometimes can't finish anything because it is never good enough. So I now strive not for perfection, but for good enough. In doing things "good enough," things actually get done. And I am grateful for this new perspective that good enough really is good enough!

## 187

I concentrate on the good stuff. I put abundance, gratitude, and appreciation in the front of my mind every day.

## 188

I believe in and trust my wisdom. It is sometimes wise to seek advice from others, and in the end, the decisions are up to me.

## 189

I am a good person. I believe and appreciate this about me.

## 190

I face the fear, I acknowledge the fear,
I embrace the fear, and I move ahead
in spite of the fear.

## 191

I accept no more self-doubts. I appreciate
and am worthy of all the great things that
are happening in my life.

## 192

I choose to step outside my comfort zone
and try new things, savoring the process
and not worrying about the outcome.

## 193

I am grateful you are in my life! You can love a lot of different people for a lot of different reasons: a partner, a friend, a child, a parent. Remember to let the people you love know that you love them, and why. If you are grateful they are in your life, let them know! As long as you are sincere, there is no such thing as saying it too much!

## 194

I do my best, and that is enough for me.

## 195

I am a conduit for loving energy – sending it and receiving it at all times.

## 196

I choose to see and celebrate
the abundance and beauty that
exist in the world.

## 197

We are all connected. What hurts one
hurts us all; what helps one helps us all.
I do my part to take care of the world
by taking care of me.

## 198

I am worthy just the way I am,
right here and now.

## 199

Today, I do my best to live MY life.
I avoid comparisons with others. I avoid
all expectations. I do my best, and that
is enough. I remember that I am here to
be the best me that I can be, and I leave
others to be the best that they can be.
I appreciate what I have, and have
gratitude for what I can do. I practice
forgiveness and revel in the possibilities.

## 200

I create an environment that supports me.
I am inspired and strengthened by
the comfort I feel in this space.

make room for bliss

## 201

I am a creative force of endless possibilities. I am limited only by myself, and only if I choose to be.

## 202

Life is something I do, not something that happens to me. I appreciate each new day I am given, and celebrate it to the best of my ability.

## 203

I let go of my fear and lean into the moment. I believe in and expect wonderful things, and I appreciate what I already have. I think BIG!

## 204

I am pure powerful energy,
gratefully living a life of abundance.

## 205

It's good to know that all things are possible. It's also good to remember that they may not happen in my time frame, exactly when I would want them to. Things happen when they are supposed to happen, and I am grateful for that.

make room for bliss

## 206

The choices I make in life are mine,
and I take responsibility for them.

## 207

I am centered in truth and understanding
and light. I maintain my center,
no matter what is happening to me.

## 208

I appreciate and listen to the opinions
of others, and when it is time to make a
decision, I consider what I have heard,
keep counsel with my intuition,
and make up my own mind. I know
what is right for me.

## 209

Today I go out in the world and hold my head up. I do not worry about the past or what people are thinking of me. I take responsibility for what I am responsible for, and I let go of anything I have no control over. I remember that everyone does not have to like me, and that I don't have to like everyone else. I treat everyone with respect.

## 210

I am kindness and love. Unfortunately, there are times when the tragedy of current events causes me heartache. I do not allow myself to become numb. I am not helpless. I begin each day with a renewed intention to show kindness and love.

## 211

I dance through life, celebrating the unexpected that makes me sidestep to the left or right before I move on. A step backwards is just a part of the dance, and I embrace it all enthusiastically.

## 212

I ask for help when I need it, and I appreciate the help that I receive.

## 213

I am a willing and enthusiastic participant in life.

## 214

Today, I give myself time and permission to do the things that are right for me to do. I make sure that I am on my path, even if searching for that path IS my path. And by doing so I am, in a way, giving everyone else the space and time and permission to do the same.

## 215

I am…full of possibility.

## 216

I listen to my inner voice; I trust in what I hear; I believe in my truth.

## 217

I release perfectionism and embrace enough! Sometimes being fully present in the moment means a whole slew of other stuff doesn't get done right now. With intention and communication it can get done eventually, and I choose to be okay with that.

## 218

I celebrate where I am. I am further along on my journey than I was yesterday, and not as far as I will be tomorrow. I stop to celebrate where I am right now, this very minute, for I know this is where I am supposed to be. I learn my lessons, love my people, and appreciate the abundance around me.

## 219

I am…resilient.

## 220

Not only do I believe in the goodness of others, I believe in the goodness of ME.

## 221

Tapping into the core of who I am as a human being helps me to be grounded, centered, and focused. I am solid and flexible at the same time, like a tree that is firmly rooted to the earth and can also dance in the wind.

make room for bliss

## 222

I am enough. When things are tough,
I am enough. When things get
overwhelming, I am enough. When
I feel totally inadequate, I am enough.
At all times, I am enough.

## 223

I live in the now. The past is done, and I can't, nor do I want to, go back there. The future has not yet happened, and I will not base my life on potential events that may or may not occur. The only time I have is now, and I live each moment of it fully.

## 224

I listen to my body to learn its messages.

## 225

I am grateful for what I have and am NOW!

## 226

I believe in miracles and magic. When I start to forget this, the easiest way back to it is to be around a baby. How can you be around babies and NOT believe in miracles and magic?

## 227

I deserve to be happy!

make room for bliss

## 228

I am a survivor. What happens to me does not define who I am or who I want to be. When I stumble, I recover. When I fall, I get up. I seek out the resources I need to continue on my journey.

## 229

Power runs through me like a current in the flowing river. I can believe it is there or not – that is my choice. But whether I believe it or not, it is always there. I can acknowledge and use it, or I can fight against it, or I can ignore it. I choose to acknowledge and use my power.

## 230

I do the best I can with the information that I have at the moment. I adjust as I get new information. I will not beat myself up over my mistakes – real or perceived.
I am a competent person.

## 231

I am grateful for everything that happens in my life. I choose to learn the lessons provided in each circumstance, and then move on.

## 232

I honor my process and
embrace my resilience.

## 233

I live in gratitude. There is so much to
be grateful for in my life: from the small
to the large, from the day-to-day
to the once-in-a-lifetime.

## 234

I am strong, vibrant, loving energy. I stand
up for myself, and for others who cannot
stand up for themselves. I embrace both
my feminine and masculine sides, for they
are both a part of me. I appreciate my
uniqueness, even while celebrating that
I am connected to all.

## 235

I have the power to change my life,
and I will use it.

## 236

I believe. I believe that the work I do today is getting me to where I want to be. I believe that angels are watching over me. I believe that good things are coming. I believe in doing the right thing, even when it is the hard thing. I believe in people. I believe that the Universe is conspiring to aid me on my journey.
I believe that I make a difference.
**I BELIEVE.**

## 237

I am a legacy changer!
I dwell in possibility.

## 238

I joyfully dance through the sun
and the rain, for I know that I am loved!

## 239

I accept that I am a work in progress, and that there will be bumps along this road. At times I may react to things differently than I would like to; that is okay. I make corrections as I go, and recognize that this journey is ongoing. I do the best I can, and I trust the process.

## 240

I am resilient; I will bounce back;
this does not define me.

## 241

I choose to live with gratitude
and appreciation for all that
I have and will have.

## 242

I embrace all aspects of myself,
the dark as well as the light.
I am my own best friend.

make room for bliss

## 243

I am not who I was yesterday. I learn from my successes and my failures, and I move on. Today is a new day; I decide who and what I am, unencumbered by my past.

## 244

Today I love and accept everyone for who and what they are, right now. I understand that everyone is evolving, and many are trying to be better tomorrow than today, including me. I appreciate and celebrate that, and I do not wait until tomorrow to love and accept everyone – I love and accept everyone NOW.

## 245

The fact that your path is not the same as my path does not take away from either path. I celebrate you on your path, and me on mine.

## 246

I am content to let things unfold in their own time, as I know they surely will.

## 247

I embrace all that I am; I am worthy now.

## 248

I strive to do the best that I can, at all times. When I stumble, I pick myself up. When I fall short, I begin anew.
The journey is mine, and I embrace it.

## 249

I am alive and well, living my life with massive gratitude for the abundance with which I have been bestowed. Joy, laughter, love, and play are part of my everyday experiences. I embrace life!

## 250

I radiate pure energy and sparkling love where ever I go.

## 251

The past is just that – the past. I remember and learn from and appreciate the past. That doesn't mean that I hang on to the past. My life is not in the past, nor is it in the future. My life is in the present, and that is where I live – in the present. The past does not own me.

## 252

I am…a legacy maker.

## 253

I greet each day with a happy heart and appreciation for the abundance I have been blessed with.

## 254

Today is the day! Today is the only day that I have, and I am going to squeeze every last drop of living out of it. I revel in its energy, and partake of its abundance.

## 255

I am doing the best that I can with the information and the resources that I have right now. Everything is good.

## 256

Enough. There is enough, I have enough, I AM enough. Enough said.

## 257

I send healing energy to the earth
and all who live on it.

## 258

I am only just beginning.
I am not yet where I want to be,
but I am further than I was yesterday.
My potential is limitless!

## 259

I appreciate happiness, joy, and laughter,
and participate in them daily.

## 260

I do all that I can today, as good
as I can today, and that is enough.

## 261

I am love and light, able to maneuver any dark moment while holding space for myself to be important. Today is the day that under no circumstances will I be self-deprecating.

## 262

I cultivate ease in my life. I believe in having faith. I also believe in proactively educating myself so that the unknown can become a learning process. Taking action to learn more calms and prepares me, so that I can make more informed choices.

## 263

I strive to be the best I can be, and
am happy with who I am right now!
I celebrate all the parts of me!

## 264

I am one with everything in the Universe;
I am one with the Universe itself.

## 265

Good things are happening all the time,
and they are happening to me.

## 266

I have the power not only to decide to
change my life, but indeed to change it.
No one else gets to decide; it is up to me.
I make the decision, and I do the work.

make room for bliss

### 267

I am content that I am doing the best that I can now, as I strive to do better every day.

### 268

Tomorrow will happen as it is supposed to, whether I worry myself sick over it or not. Yesterday is already done, and nothing I do today can change what has already happened. I choose to embrace each and every one of today's moments, one at a time, appreciating being present in them.

## 269

Just for today, I will be totally in the moment, present to all that is happening, taking it all in. I will not worry about tomorrow; I will not dwell on yesterday. This will be my first thought each day upon waking.

## 270

I am creative, capable, resourceful, and whole; I live my life accordingly.

## 271

I remember to take care of myself.

## 272

Today is a great day!

## 273

I am so grateful for what I have and what I am going to have. I embrace everything in my life; the things that I learn from, as well as the things I love. It is all good, and it is all appreciated.

## 274

It is my life; they are my decisions. You don't have to understand or like them, but you do have to let me make them. I may not make the same choice that you would, but I will make the best choice that I can with the information I have at the time. And the fact that I made a different choice than you would have does not mean that I am rejecting you, it just means that I am not you – I am me.

## 275

I appreciate everyday luxuries;
I have clean drinking water
and that is a blessing.

## 276

I am in charge of my life; I make my choices and live with the consequences.

## 277

I remember the past and I plan for the future, but I live in the present.

## 278

I believe in Abundance. I love it and rejoice when others succeed, because I know that someone else's success does not mean there is less success for me. There is enough of everything to go around!

## 279

I am…intrepid.

## 280

A new day, brimming with endless possibilities, is starting now! I am super-excited to wrap myself up in it.

affirmations

## 281

I have a good relationship with my
intuition, because I know when the
voice inside me speaks, it is just
a more-knowing me.

## 282

I am...accepted and accepting.

## 283

Today all of my actions are made with the
best intention and to the best of my ability.
Then I let it go, with no thought of what
others think of me. If I have done my best,
with good intention, it is enough.

## 284

Times may be tough; I may have to face things that I do not want to face. I can and I will do it, because as tough as things are, I am tougher!

## 285

I am working on myself – getting clearer every day. I am patient with myself for any setbacks and bumps I encounter on my path.

## 286

Imagine this: we all acknowledge our power and put it to use in the world for good. What great things we accomplish when we do this!

*affirmations*

## 287

I woke up this morning, and that is enough reason to be grateful for this glorious day!

## 288

I am…ridiculously excited about life.

My own *Bliss*

make room for bliss

affirmations

reflections

### 289

Love is…being there.

### 290

Maybe it is time to tackle that new thing.
Be willing to be a beginner, to not be
able to do it perfectly at the start.
Persevere, and see where you end up.

### 291

Fun – a feeling created
when playful actions meet
appreciation and gratitude.

# 292

Sometimes giving up is really just letting go and moving on. When things aren't working out, it may be the way the Universe is telling you that it is time to move on, time to spend your energy on something else. For some people this may be an easy distinction to make; others may struggle with it. I do believe that life is not meant to be a struggle, that it can be easy. I also believe that sometimes you do have to get through the hard parts to get to the good parts. And I guess for right now, balancing those beliefs is what I am meant to be doing.

make room for bliss

## 293

Do you tend to over-think things? If so, we invite you to slow down and actually stop thinking for a bit. Trust your instincts, intuition, inner voice, or whatever you call it, do what you need to do, or don't do what you don't need to do, and let it go. Sometimes you need to stop thinking so hard.

## 294

Ask for what you need. Don't expect people to know what you need, and then get upset because they didn't guess right. People can't read your mind any more than you can read their minds. I used to think that asking for what I need would make me high-maintenance, which is the last thing I want. Now I realize that asking for what I need actually makes it easier for others, as they no longer need to spend time and energy trying to figure it out. Try it.

## 295

What do you say is important to you? Now look to see where you spend your time and energy – what do your actions say is important to you? If they are the same, then you are living a congruent life – what you say and what you do are in sync. If they are not the same, don't beat yourself up over it. You may want, however, to take a good look at the differences between what you say and what you do. Determine what it would take to become congruent; do you need to adjust your thinking about what is important to you, or perhaps adjust how you spend your time so that it is more in line with what you think? Don't listen to what others say should be important to you; it may be different for them, and there are no 'shoulds.' It takes a lot of energy to live a life that is not congruent. Getting your beliefs and actions in line with each other may actually lead to an easier life.

## 296

How would you spend your time if there were no barriers? Figure out a way to spend your time doing that.

## 297

Things change, and they are going to change whether you like it or not. And sometimes you will like it, and sometimes you won't. You can choose to fight the change. Or you can choose to go with the change – find the magic in it, hard as it may be to identify. In the end, the change is going to happen whichever way you choose to approach it. So what do you choose?

298

Just because you can,
doesn't mean you should.

299

Be open...to new people, new ideas, new situations, new possibilities. You don't have to act on everything new that comes along; new isn't always better than old. But old isn't always better than new, either. Be open to everything that life has to offer – then decide what you want from a place of choice.

# 300

Put your Attention on your Intention and see what you Manifest! What do you spend your time thinking about? Do you have a clear intention of where you want to be? Do you put your attention on what you want? If you don't really know what you want or where you want to be, it may be difficult to get there. Or, even if you get there, it may be difficult to realize that you ARE there. We would invite you to think about what you really want, set your Intention, and then put your Attention on it.

# 301

Family isn't always about blood. Sometimes family is about finding your tribe – the people who get you, who are there for you. You have a family of birth, and they can be very important in your life. And don't forget that you also have a family of choice. Your family of choice can augment your family of birth, or replace it, or anything in between. A family of choice is what you need it to be. Celebrate all your families!

*reflections*

## 302

What if…? What if you believed in yourself? What if you didn't worry about what other people think? What if you really listened to your inner voice? What if you voiced your gratitude? What if you really believed in abundance? What if…?

## 303

Be done when you know you are done. Walking away doesn't necessarily mean you are quitting. Sometimes it just means that you are done. It may be a sign that it is time to leave if you are no longer learning anything from the situation, or if you no longer like the person you are when you are in that situation. It doesn't mean that you are bad, or that other people involved are bad. It may mean that you have gotten what you need from the situation, and it is time to move on. Change is hard; you may have to overcome fear of the unknown. And if you want to continue to grow, you need to know when it is time to leave.

304

Before you jump to action, we would invite you to take a pause. Become aware of all that is, so that you can know what you want to do. Awareness comes first.

# 305

Do good. Do as much good as you can, whatever your circumstances. If that means you send $100,000 to a charity you support – great. If that means you buy coffee for the guy behind you in line – also great. If that means you help elderly neighbors by mowing their lawn or carrying in their groceries – great as well. If all the good you have in you today is to smile at someone on the street – that is enough. Volunteer, be helpful, be nice. Just do what you can, when you can. It all makes a difference in this world.

# 306

What if it didn't have to be hard? What will happen if you just lean into the fear and do it? Does it really have to be difficult to

make it worthwhile? What if that is just
an old belief that you are clinging to?
What would happen in your life if
you embraced a new belief?

## 307

You get more of what you want when
you are grateful for what you have.

## 308

When things get tough, when you're
not feeling 100%, when you just feel out
of sorts....listen to your body. Find your
'RESET' button, and push it. Maybe
it's taking a walk, getting some fresh air,
or being alone for 5 minutes.
Whatever it is – do it.

reflections

## 309

Do you ever get stuck because making a choice feels permanent? But is it? It may be easier to make a decision if you can see that it is not necessarily permanent; you can make a course correction down the road if needed. That doesn't mean making a choice will be easy, only that it is possible. And sometimes that is all you need to realize in order to move forward.

## 310

Are you using the past to understand your present, or to avoid it? Looking to the past to help you understand your present can be a healthy thing. It is important, however, to be sure that you are not looking to the past to avoid your present.

# 311

What are you waiting for? Is there something that you want to do, but you keep convincing yourself that the time is not right or conditions are not perfect so you can't do it yet? Think about this: in a year, a year will have passed whether or not you pursue your dream. Do your due diligence, but don't let perfectionism stand in the way of taking a step toward what you want. Ask yourself what are you waiting for, and is it worth it to wait?

## 312

Sometimes taking things to the next level means stepping outside your comfort zone. Classical musician? What about learning to play jazz? Contemporary dancer? What about a circus acrobatics class? What would inject new energy into what you do?

## 313

What floats your boat? What makes you feel alive and loved? What makes you feel needed? Whatever it is, go out and do it. If you can't make a living doing it, then find another way to fit it into your life. Do it in an official capacity, or just go around your town spreading the love in your own unique way.

## 314

You can't live someone else's life for them.
Everyone has to make their own choices,
make their own mistakes, and live with
their own consequences. And yes, you
have to let them. If someone has a lesson
to learn, they are going to have to learn it.
Sometimes the hardest thing in life is
to just stand by and be as supportive
as you can.

## 315

There is always something to look forward
to. Like in the garden, the blossoms of life
come in phases. Be glad, because it means
there is always something to look forward
to and be grateful for.

# 316

Don't let the fear of making a mistake stop you from doing something. There are very few mistakes that cannot be overcome; go ahead and make that decision and see where it leads. If it leads to something you wanted, that is good. If it leads to something you didn't want, that is also good. Finding what you don't want helps you figure out what you do want, so it might be argued that the mistake that brought you what you don't want also brought you closer to the knowledge of what you do want – and that's a good thing. So don't fear mistakes, embrace them!

make room for bliss

## 317

Eye contact: Where the deepest of emotions can be shared, the human spirit can be honored, and respect can be exchanged. No words needed.

## 318

Things don't always turn out the way we expect them to. However, they do always turn out the way they are meant to. You may not realize the reason for a short while, or even for a long while. Whatever the outcome, be open to the possibilities!

## 319

Your path isn't always straightforward. Sometimes it takes a turn you don't expect, or presents you with a detour that you must take. Don't worry; trust that you will get to where you need to be, and carry on. And remember – it really is more about the journey than the destination, so enjoy your travels.

## 320

Everyone deserves some patience and a smile. Some people are very good at holding their emotions inside and going about their daily lives. You may not know that the man who bumped into you got some bad news just five minutes ago, or that the woman who seemed to glare at you is just trying to keep from crying until she gets to her car. Everyone is going through something, and everyone deserves your patience and a smile. Try to remember this when you are out and about – you may just make someone's day with that smile of yours.

321

You can say a lot of things, but what people will remember is what you do. It is true that actions speak louder than words. Are your words and actions aligned? Do you say one thing, but do another? Take a minute to think – what do your actions say about you?

## 322

Love is…honoring boundaries.

## 323

Are you feeling overwhelmed? Is there too much to do, and not enough time in which to do it? Are you doing something new, and you don't quite have the natural rhythm of it yet? Instead of berating yourself for it, try asking yourself one question: Are you doing the best you can? If you can honestly answer yes, then cut yourself some slack, because your best is the best you can do. Your best is enough.

## 324

Remember, though the noise may imply otherwise, there is much more good than evil in this world. Drown out the evil not with more noise, but with appreciation of the abundance, compassion, love, and hope that fill our world.

## 325

Do you ever wonder what you can do for a friend who is hurting or in confusion? It is natural to want to do something, and by all means be sure to ask what they need. And sometimes the best thing we can do is to hold space for each other so we can heal and figure things out.

# 326

The fact that things have always been a certain way does not mean that they always have to stay that way. This applies to many things, from your morning routine to your relationships. Challenge your assumptions. Assuming that something is true may indeed make it true for you. Do you assume that you can't find time to write? Maybe you can't find 3 hours to sit and write, but maybe you can eke out 30 minutes here and there to put pen to paper. Do you assume that since your relationship with someone has not been great for a decade that it can't be better? Reach out in small ways and see if things change. Do you assume that your always-chaotic mornings can never change?

make room for bliss

Try doing something differently and see if it makes a difference. Do you assume you can't dance? Try taking a lesson and seeing if the issue is that you don't know how, not that you can't. We are not promising that everything will change; we are saying that if you don't challenge the assumption that it can't, it won't.

### 327

The only way to get from here to there is a step at a time. It doesn't matter where or what 'here' and 'there' are – it's always the same. To make progress, put one foot in front of the other and take that next step.

## 328

To be gracious is to honor the humanity in others, not necessarily to do what someone else wants you to do. Being a witness to someone's life, and acknowledging their thoughts and feelings, can go a long way. Consider being flexible when it feels like a growing experience, while staying true and holding steadfast if it feels like you are compromising your core morals and values. Rock on!

## 329

Strive to live your life mindfully and in the present. A lot of people say it, and it is true: yesterday is gone, tomorrow is not here yet, all we have is now. If you are always worrying about the past or the future, you are not able to be present for the now. In this super-hectic, highly technological world, there is always something that wants our attention, often pulling us out of now. Resist that pull. Now is worth being present for.

## 330

When something happens to you, good or bad, it is hard not to react immediately to it. It can be a wise thing to take a minute and think about it. Perhaps ask yourself, "What feels important about this right now?" Remember, life is not so much about what happens to you as it is about how you react to what happens to you.

# 331

At the end of the day, all you really have is how you were in the world today. Ask yourself how you did, and try to answer without judgment. If the answer is, "I spent my day being me, acting as I want to be, and not in reaction to what was around me," then pat yourself on the back and try to do even better tomorrow. If the answer is, "I spent some of my day in reaction to what was around me, not being true to myself," then pat yourself on the back for doing the best you could, and try to do better tomorrow.

## 332

Today is a gift to you. It is a clean slate; nothing from the past clings to it, unless you decide it does. What are you going to do with this lovely gift?

## 333

Who gets to decide? When it comes to your life and what you think and do and feel, who is ultimately responsible? You make your own decisions, and you are responsible for the consequences of those decisions. So as much as you might like to think it is not up to you, it really is. And you may not always get to decide what happens next, but you do always get to decide how you react to what happens next.

## 334

Sometimes in the midst of chaos, it's good to take a step back, disconnect, and ask this important question: What is my lesson here? Instead of trying to find who is to blame, and feeling like a victim, choose to use the experience to learn something.

## 335

Love is…second chances.

## 336

Remember, it is not the destination that matters, but rather, the journey. There are a million ways to get from A to B: the fast way, the slow way, the scenic way, the way of many lessons. And none of those ways is THE right way – there is no one right way. Or maybe the reality is that they are all the right way. Each way is the right way for someone, at some point in their life. Your mission, should you decide to accept it, is to savor your journey, and learn all that you can from it. And, if at some point you decide this is no longer the path you choose to be on, then choose another.

## 337

Life is too short for regrets. You don't know if you have 2 minutes or 20 years left in your life. Decide what you are going to do, then do it. When you look back on it, see the lesson in it. Don't waste your time wishing you had chosen differently, regretting how things turned out. Rejoice in the fact that you are aware enough to appreciate all the lessons in your life.

## 338

Love is…sharing your chocolate.

### 339

Sometimes it feels so good to just let go of something. Are you hanging onto something – a job, a tradition, a friendship – because it sometimes feels easier to go with what you know than to move on to something new? Make sure you are sticking with things because there is something there for you, not because you are afraid of what you will have if you let it go. Remember, to receive something new, you may have to say goodbye to something old.

### 340

What kind of energy
are you sending out?

## 341

You know that moment when something ends and something new begins? Some people call it transition. That's fine, but when I think of it as an opportunity to create, I just feel differently. I think I will give it a silly made up name...Creatunity anyone? Rock on!

## 342

What is important for you to do today? Whether it is to tell someone you love them, pick up a phone to call someone you haven't talked to for a while, take a nap, read a book, or get something specific done, make sure you do it. It doesn't matter if anyone else thinks it is important, if it's important to you, do it.

## 343

Making a decision may mean making a change. Change is an opportunity to evolve your legacy. Acknowledge your feelings during these times. Whether you need to grieve the change or to celebrate it, do it. You are creating your life one decision at a time, and your life matters.

## 344

In order to move forward, you must be willing to fail. How do you find out what DOES work? You eliminate what you find out does NOT work. Failure moves you forward.

## 345

I am grateful for so much. Even the tough decisions I have to make are cause for gratitude, for they mean that I have things from which to choose. It's a beautiful sunny day, and I am extremely grateful for that; if it were rainy, I would also be grateful for that. My attitude is one of gratitude, for whatever comes my way.

## 346

If you can't stop talking about it, you're not over it. You can't move on until you have let the past go, so do what you must to deal with it, and let it go. Sometimes that means talking to the person in question; sometimes it means coming to grips with the fact that you can't right a wrong. Sometimes it is enough to sit in silence and feel your feelings, and then say goodbye to them. Whatever it is, do it and then be done with it.

Sometimes this is all you need to consider: Is it necessary and is it kind?

# 348

What's important to you? Do you say one thing, and your actions show something else? Are you still saying that something is important to you because it used to be? Things change; we change. What was the most important to you 5 years ago may no longer hold that top spot in your current life; it may not even make the list now. Be honest with yourself about your priorities, and don't let someone else decide for you what is the most important thing to you.

## 349

The jewels aren't always strewn on top of the ground, and answers and feelings aren't always apparent at first glance. Sometimes you have to dig to get to the treasure.

## 350

Sometimes we're running from demons that no longer exist. How long has it been since you really sized up the life you have now? Is it possible that you've made it to the other side and didn't even know it? If so, mark today as a new chapter in your story.

# 351

Letting go is NOT the same as giving up. Sometimes you have to be willing to let something go because it is dragging you down, or you have chosen to change your focus. Life goes on, and your dream to be a ballerina may morph into a dream to be a choreographer – or a fisherman! This does not mean that you have given up; it may mean that you have chosen to move ahead. How do you know if you are giving up or letting go? Listen to your heart (or inner voice or whatever you want to call it). And remember, letting go of something right now may mean that you are walking away from it forever, but it may just mean that you are putting it on the back burner for now. It's your life – you get to choose.

make room for bliss

## 352

Avoid letting spite become a part of your decision. Spite is not about the other person. It is about you letting anger become your fuel, and your actions robbing you of your divine purpose. Love and light can fill the darkest places.

## 353

There is a reason for everything that happens to me, though I may not always see it at the time. Every situation is a learning experience; sometimes I am the teacher and sometimes I am the student. I appreciate the way everything fits together. It's all good.

## 354

Love is…listening.

## 355

Too many things troubling your mind? Are you discovering that you have no control over some things? Maybe it's time to realize that you really have no control over anything but your own mind. Control over anything else is an illusion. Maybe it's time to let go of the illusion…

## 356

Decisions are not about perfection.
They are choices that we make with the
information we have at the time.
Be mindful and intentional, and follow
through. That is what doing your
best is about.

## 357

What is important to you? Look at how
you spend your time, and see if it matches
what you say. Because how you spend your
time is a pretty good indication of what
is truly important to you, even if you don't
realize it. It is not always easy to make
what you say and what you do match up.
And the first step is realizing that
they either do or do not.

reflections

# 358

The world is going to tell you a lot things – this is most important; no, pay attention to this; you HAVE to do this first. Ignore it all, and listen to that small voice inside you; it won't steer you wrong. What the world needs right now is people who listen to their inner voice and do what is right for them to do right now. Making this world a better place is going to happen because a lot of people do a lot of little things when it is right to do them.

Listen to your inner voice!

## 359

Remember this: there is always hope. When you are at the lowest point and can't seem to find anything to look forward to, when even the light at the end of the tunnel appears to be a train, there is still hope. When you are so low that you don't even know what it is you are hoping for, reach out to a friend and let them hold that hope for you. THERE IS ALWAYS HOPE!

## 360

It is important to remember that you never really lose your power. You may feel like you have lost your power, but it is your connection to your power that you have temporarily forgotten. And you can and will regain that connection, and once again step into your power.

## 361

Living your life differently does not mean that you are living your life wrong.

## 362

The words you use are important – especially the ones you use with yourself. Remember to be at least as gentle with yourself as you are with others.

## 363

Resourcefulness: some people seem to have it in spades, but when you get down to it, being resourceful is a learned skill. Sometimes it is a force of circumstance, sometimes we seek it because we recognize its potential. Either way, expect to grow as you go.

## 364

Today, I have the hard conversations and live my life with authenticity, to the best of my ability. And then I get up tomorrow and do the same. It is not about the outcome, it is about the effort.

## 365

At the end of the day, when all is said and done, what is important?

reflections

# My own *Bliss*

make room for bliss

reflections

# about the authors

JUDY STOFFEL LOEWEN lives in Seattle, WA, where she is a bassoon playing Life Coach who does some editing on the side. Her husband and adult son are great at giving her a hard time and keeping her laughing.

In addition to thinking up Bliss, KRISTIE KELLER is grateful to be pursuing a variety of delights she refers to as her life's work. These include, but are not limited to, being a wife and mother, working as a licensed massage practitioner, and staying up way too late to indulge her love of learning.

Judy Stoffel Loewen
Certified Professional Coach, InviteChange
Associate Certified Coach, International Coach Federation

Kristie Keller
Licensed Massage Practitioner

www.makeroomforbliss.com
www.facebook.com/makeroomforbliss